2017

TRIGGERED
FHHUCK!
NOOOO!
FEMIN
SCHROEDER '17

I FIND it REALLY Hard to think that anyone out there takes me seriously As a NON FORM Gender CON ING PERSON
ONE WAY
SCHROEDER '17

SURVIVOR
BACKWARD
SCHROEDER'17

Blah
blah blah
GENDER
blah
SEX
blah
blah
GENDER
SEX
blah
blah
blah
bl ah
SEX
Blah
blah
GENDER
Blah
Gender is a Performance
So why not put on a Show?
SCHROEDER '17

You are a Fucking piece of Fucking shit!
You're Fucking TRASH!
you're a FUCKING SNITCH!!!!
FUCK YOU!
LOVE TRUMPS HATE
SCHROEDER '17

Patriarchy runs the world
check your white Male Privilege!
SCHROEDER '17

You know the CAT has FEELINGS - and it makes it so much harder to be ANGRY!
When they scratch your arm when they SPRAWL every ounce of themselves on your BODY!
Meow.
When they BEG 'n' BEG for something you CANNOT GIVE you just wish it would CLAW and TAKE bcuz eventually you will say —— YES!
SCHROEDER '17

We're the other 98% of whatever. It's very SAD!
PUSSY NOT FOR GRABS
THIS PUSSY BITES FOR OUR RIGHTS
SCHROEDER '17

I see the Future
The Future is nasty!
SCHROEDER '17

NASTY
AND
WE ARE HERE to be NASTY!
PROUD
We are Here to be RESPECTED
SCHROEDER '17

SHUT THE
I'M NOT HERE TO LISTEN TO YOU
SPEW YOUR JESUS SHIT!
SLUT
FUCK UP!
SCHROEDER '17

Do you like apples AND bananas?
HELL NO BITCH!
BISEXUAL
SCHROEDER '17

REFUGEES WELCOME AT MY PLACE!
SCHROEDER '17

Jiggaboo
Uncle
Tom
Ass
Niggas
SCHROEDER'17

DIE
CIS
SCUM
SCHROEDER '17

KEEP YER HEALTH
FOOD OFF
THIS CAMPUS
KEEP YER HEALTH
FOOD OFF THIS
CAMPUS!!
SCHROEDER '17

IF YOU GET RID OF ALL
THE
MEXi
CANS
WHO WILL
CLEAN
THE
TOILETS
?
RETARD
SCHROEDER '17

THE PUCE SCREAMER

Kids don't belong to their parents or to their families
FUCK OFF
KIDS BELONG TO THE COMMUNITY!
SCHROEDER '17

BOYCOTT THE BOOB
it's unethical inappropriate and a BURDEN !!
WHAT FUCKING CRAZY LOOKS LIKE
SCHROEDER'17

KRYPTONITE
ASSHOLE
SCHROEDER'17

Filthy + PROUD
POUND PROUD
EMPOWERED
SCHROEDER '17

I'M SORRY!!
HE WILL NOT DIVIDE US

MY SEX JUNK'S
BETTER
THAN
BAGEL
WITH
LOX
WITH
LOTS OF
SCHMEAR
MMMM.
SCHROEDER '17

BABY MAN
SCHROEDER '17

MINE!
I FEEL
VIOLATED
SCHROEDER'17

When i grow up i wanna be a FASCIST CULT LEADER
by ANY MEANNESS NECESSARY...
HATE...
FEAR
LIES...
BANN
SHUT DOWN FREE SPEECH
SCHROEDER '17

ROYAL HIGHNESS
Princess
VICTIMIZATION NATION
SCHROEDER '17
I'M SURROUNDED BY HUMAN GARBAGE!

THIS IS A GOOD MOVE   THIS IS A GOOD MOVE
THIS IS A GOOD MOVE
THIS IS A GOOD MOVE
THIS IS A GOOD MOVE
THIS IS A GOOD MOVE
THIS IS A GOOD MOVE
THIS IS A GOOD MOVE
THIS A GOOD MOVE
THIS IS A GOOD MOVE
NO!
YESSSS
SCHROEDER '17
BRILLIANT BOLD BRAVE
OR JUST PLAIN STUPID

"the revolution isn't fucking easy!"
MY BODY MY CHOICE
SCHROEDER '17

A is for ALLEPO
B is for BUSH
C is for... C is for? is for??
RUSSIA!
SCHROEDER '17

SOMEONE MISSED A FEEDING!
I'M WITH ME
SCHROEDER '14

AHHHHHHHH
A
H
SCHROEDER'17

I hate You BCUZ UR A WHITE MALE!
Yr a Missognist pig!
K. SCHROEDER '17

o o o o o oBservant
little cuck!
YOU'RE A FUCKING
WHITE MALE!

IM FUCKING BETTER THAN YOU!!
YOU ARE GARBAGE!
YOU ARE A PIECE OF SHIT!
I am a Social Justice Warrior!
and you are FUCKING DUMB!!
bitch!
K.SCHROEDER'17

I'LL SUCK A DICK IF I WANNA
SUCK A DICK!
I SUCK GREAT DICK BY THE WAY BUT NOT YERS YER
UGLY!
SCHROEDER '17